The Little Book of

PHOBIAS

The Little Book of

PHOBiAS

*An Unflinching Look
at Our Deepest Fears, with
More Than 250 Quotations
From Life and Literature*

**Compiled by
Joe Kohut**

R U N N I N G   P R E S S
PHILADELPHIA, PENNSYLVANIA

Canadian representatives: General Publishing Co., Ltd.,
30 Lesmill Road, Don Mills, Ontario M3B 2T6.

9 8 7 6 5 4 3 2 1
Digit on the right indicates the number of this printing.

ISBN: 1-56138-297-3

Library of Congress Cataloging-in Publication Number 93-85514

Conceived by Rachael Hayes Teacher
Cover design by Toby Schmidt
Interior design by Nancy Loggins
Interior illustrations by Robert Meganck
Typography by Deborah Lugar
Printed and bound in U.S.A.

This book may be ordered by mail from the publisher.
Please add $2.50 for postage and handling. *But try your bookstore first!*

Running Press Book Publishers
125 South Twenty-second Street
Philadelphia, Pennsylvania 19103-4399

For Butch and Maggie

CONTENTS

introduction

In the opening lines of his *Anti-Memoirs*, André Malraux recounts a wartime conversation with the parish priest of the little town of Drome in southeastern France. The area was one of the principal strongholds of the Maquis during the Second World War. The priest had escaped with Malraux from a prison camp in 1940 and was now serving as chaplain to the resistance fighters in the area.

As they talked into the night, Malraux asked the priest what he had learned about the human condition after hearing the confessions of his parishioners for some fifteen years.

After some thought, the burly curé replied that "the fundamental fact is that there is no such thing as a grown-up person."

There are some who contend that phobias are shards of childhood experience that are lodged deep in that part of our interior life that will never grow up. Others argue that these terrors are spawned in a psychic pool that we share with other members of our species. Still others claim that phobias spring from that shadow land that bridges the temporal world and the realm of the unconscious. Whatever their origin, they are a part of the human experience that is as ancient as dragons or demons and as current as HIV.

Phobias can trigger a sense of dread and terror that is constrained by neither gender nor geography. They can loose a fear and loathing worthy of a Kierkegaard or a Hunter S. Thompson. Phobias are just as likely to haunt the occupants of a pricey pied-à-terre as they are the residents of a homeless shelter.

The name we have for these exaggerated and illogical fears has its roots in the Greek *phebesthai*: to flee, to fear. The irony here is that phobias are terrors that, by definition, we carry within us, and that makes flight a difficult proposition at best. Phobias belong to that class of phenomena from which we can run but we just can't hide.

And while we can't hide, we can talk about them. Our deepest fears continue to serve as grist for novels, biographies, letters, movies, and the stories that we tell around the electronic campfire by way of the satellite dish. In this way we try to manage our fears and create a shared record of the things we dread. This volume was created in an effort to expand that record.

And, just for the record, high places give me the willies.

THE *15* MOST COMMON
FEARS AND PHOBIAS

According to a study conducted by the Anxiety Disorder Association of America the following have been identified as the 15 most common fears of men and women in the U.S. While men and women share the same 15, the way they rank them varies. In order to be included in the list the fear or anxiety had to present "more than an inconvenience" in daily life.

FEAR	*RANKING:*	
	WOMEN	*MEN*
Spiders, bugs, mice, snakes, and bats	1	2
Heights	2	1
Taking public transportation	3	5
Afraid of being in water	4	6
Storms	5	11
Being in a crowd	6	3
Miscellaneous fear	7	4
Confinement in an enclosed space	8	8
Being in/on tunnels and bridges	9	10
Speaking to an audience	10	9
Being out of the house alone	11	14
Being alone	12	13
Being near a harmless animal or a dangerous animal that cannot harm them	13	15
Meeting new people	14	7
Eating in public	15	12

Fear itself

Do not ask, Reader, how my
    blood ran cold
    and my voice choked up
    with fear. I cannot write it:
    this is a terror that cannot
    be told.

DANTE

The real horror is not in the
shadows, but in that little
twisted world inside our
own skulls.

ROBERT BLOCH

Extreme terror gives us back
the gestures of childhood.

MALCOLM DE CHAZAL

Panic is the mind's way of readying the body for fight or flight in the face of emergency. What makes panic attacks so puzzling is that they seem to come out of the blue. There is nothing to be afraid of. No external threat. Only the overpowering sensation of fear.

M. KATHERINE SHEAR
DIRECTOR OF ANXIETY DISORDER CLINIC AT NEW YORK HOSPITAL

We are more often frightened than hurt: our troubles spring more from fancy than reality.

SENECA

"I fear many things: dogs, horses, firearms, the sea, thunderstorms, machinery, the country roads at night."

"But why do you fear a bit of bread?"

"I imagine," Stephan said, "that there is a malevolent reality behind those things I say I fear."

JAMES JOYCE

Fear is the surrender of the succor that which reason offers.

APOCRYPHA: WISDOM OF SOLOMON

Fear of danger is ten times more terrifying than danger itself.

DANIEL DEFOE

It is the feeling of helplessness that is the worst part of terror, worse than the actual terror itself.

JEAN MARZOLLO

Our fears always outnumber our dangers.

LATIN PROVERB

Everyone is susceptible to major panic on occasion. It is the minor panic that is surprising; not only a sudden fear but an unreasoning one. . . . Looking back on many of them it's easy to laugh: they're ephemeral, unimportant, and frequently ridiculous. . . . But when they happen, logic doesn't apply, the heart misses a beat, the brain scrambles, and there's a little frisson that says "this can't be happening."

ENID NEMY

Fear is the result of the body assuming ascendancy over the soul. . . . Repetitive labor, the doing of one thing over and over again and always in the same way is a terrifying prospect to a certain kind of mind. It is terrifying to me.

HENRY FORD

It comes in all sorts of forms. I suppose it's always there, but most times it hovers unseen. It is an animal, a monster which hides in its foul corner without revealing itself, but you know it is there and that it may come forward at any moment . . . the dark chaos of fear.

SIR LAWRENCE OLIVIER

If fear comes from the protector, who can protect us from fear? I am still more frightened by the fearless power in the eyes of my fellow psychiatrists than by the powerless fear in the eyes of their patients. I dread the thought of either look appearing in my eyes.

R.D. LAING

Conscious or not, anguish—a fundamental anguish of being—despite our smile, strikes in the depths of all our hearts and is the undertone of all our conversation.

The enormity of space is the most tangible and thus the most frightening aspect.

PIERRE TEILHARD DE CHARDIN

There are different kinds of being scared. There is the relaxed kind, the afterscare when you get away with something dumb, get home and tied down, eat supper and are half asleep when the event marches through your mind accompanied by all the other ways it could have turned out. You could call this a review scare. The nice thing about this is that you can have it in privacy and don't have to tell about it if you don't want to.

Another kind is the flash scare. That's the scare of a sudden occurrence that comes and goes swiftly—the reaction from pilots who share it is nearly always loud laughter and loud talking: "Did you see that?"

GORDON BAXTER

All of us are born with a set of instinctive fears—of falling, of the dark, of lobsters, of falling on lobsters in the dark, of speaking before a Rotary Club, and of the words "Some assembly required."

DAVE BARRY

Dread is not a mode of fear. Rather it is the other way around: all fear finds its ground in dread. . . . That of which we are frightened can be (and most of the time is) something with which we are very well acquainted.

If, however, the threatening has the character of the utterly unfamiliar . . . then fear becomes *horror*.

MARTIN HEIDEGGER

Whoever is abandoned by hope has also been abandoned by fear; this is the meaning of the word "desperate."

ARTHUR SCHOPENHAUER

In English the word "panic" is more often applied to a crowd-reaction when fire breaks out or policemen charge, than to a lonely terror of the unknown. Once a crowd turns to run, trampling down invalids and children, no man, however courageous, can arrest the rush. There is no safety in numbers when fear strikes.

ROBERT GRAVES

Fear unhinges the will, and by unhinging the will it paralyzes the reason; thoughts are dispersed in all directions in place of being concentrated on one definite aim. Fear, again, protects the body. . . .

JOHN C. FULLER

Phobias are irrational fears. One phobic cannot look down from a height because the gulf seems to reach out and pull him with such force as to drag him over the guardrail. Another cannot walk from his house to his mailbox because the open space of the plains makes him feel as though he were going to dissolve or explode. One cannot bear to be in a room unless one door is open; another fears open doors because of the germs that may enter.

PETER GARRISON

Fear grows in the shadows.
Phobic people are haunted by
fear. The more they avoid what
they fear, the worse the phobia.
Phobia spreads to new objects
that are connected with the old.
Contamination spreads through
flight. Avoidance is a poor
response.

ELAN GOLOMB

A feeble mind, conscious of its
own feebleness, grows feebler
under that very consciousness.
As soon as the power of fear
becomes known to it, there
follows the fear of fear and on
the first perturbation, reason
abandons it.

HECTOR BERLIOZ

Scientists freely admit that though we know fear when we feel it or see its symptoms, we may never be able to measure it precisely or mark it clearly from the spectrum of emotions to which it belongs. . . . One man's frisson may be another man's stark horror or a third man's occasion for a belly laugh.

WALTER KENDRICK

Fear is that little darkroom where negatives are developed.

MICHAEL PRITCHARD

"What I truly fear is that the disease will progress to specific phobias. That is always a dread possibility. Fear of water. Fear of caterpillars. Fear of crossing bridges. Fear of dark places."

He moaned, and I found myself moaning too, not as loud, but I really felt sorry for him at that moment.

"Oh, madame," he said. "I do not wish to become phobic!"

"Who *does*?" I said, a little helplessly.

RICK DE MARINIS

. . . it [fear] is a characteristic of the American people. . . . It is rather an intellectual and spiritual fear, based on nothing tangible, and nothing which affords a reasonable basis for fear.

NELSON A. CRAWFORD

Tell us your phobia and we will tell you what you are afraid of.

ROBERT BENCHLEY

A Phobic's Lexicon

acarophobia   a fear of skin infestation by mites or ticks.

acidophobia   in plants, an inability to accommodate to acid soils.

acousticophobia   an abnormal fear of noise.

acrophobia   an abnormal fear of heights.

agoraphobia   an abnormal fear of being in crowded, public places like markets.

aichmophobia   an abnormal fear of pointed objects.

ailurophobia, aelurophobia, elurophobia, gatophobia   an abnormal fear of cats.

albuminurophobia   a fear of albumin in one's urine as a sign of kidney disease.

algophobia   an extreme fear of pain. *See also* **odynophobia**.

amathophobia   an abnormal fear of dust.

amaxophobia   an abnormal fear of riding in vehicles.

androphobia   **1.** an abnormal fear of men.
    2. a hatred of males.
anemophobia   an abnormal fear of drafts or winds.
anginophobia   an abnormal fear of quinsy or other forms of sore throat.
Anglophobia   an abnormal fear of England and things English.
anthophobia   an abnormal fear of flowers.
anthropophobia   an abnormal fear of people.

aphephobia   an abnormal fear of touching or being touched. Also called **haphephobia, haptephobia.**

arachnephobia   an abnormal fear of spiders.

asthenophobia   an abnormal fear of weakness.

astrophobia   an abnormal fear of the stars.

ataxiophobia, ataxophobia   an abnormal fear of disorder.

aurophobia   a dislike of gold.

automysophobia   an abnormal fear of being dirty.

autophobia, autophoby   an abnormal fear of being by oneself. Also called **eremiophobia, eremophobia, monophobia.**

bacillophobia   an abnormal fear of germs. Also called **bacteriophobia.**

ballistophobia   an abnormal fear of missiles.

basophobia, basiphobia   in plants, an inability to accommodate to alkaline soils.

bathmophobia   an abnormal fear of walking.

batrachophobia   an abnormal fear of frogs and toads.

belonephobia   an abnormal fear of pins and needles.

bogyphobia   an abnormal fear of demons and goblins.

bromidrosiphobia   an abnormal fear of having an unpleasant body odor.

brontophobia   an abnormal fear of thunder and thunderstorms.

cainophobia   an abnormal fear of novelty.

cardiophobia   an abnormal fear of heart disease.

cathisophobia   an abnormal fear of sitting down.

catoptrophobia   an abnormal fear of mirrors.

cherophobia   an abnormal fear of gaiety.

cholerophobia   an intense fear of cholera.

chrematophobia   an intense fear or dislike of wealth.

chromophobia   an abnormal fear of colors.

chronophobia   an abnormal discomfort concerning time.

cibophobia   an abnormal fear of food. Also called **sitophobia, sitiophobia.**

claustrophobia   an abnormal fear of confined spaces.

climacophobia   an abnormal fear of stairs.

coitophobia   an abnormal fear of sexual intercourse. Also called **cypridophobia, genophobia.**

cometophobia   an abnormal fear of comets.

coprophobia   an abnormal fear of excrement.

cremnophobia   an abnormal fear of precipices.

crystallophobia   an abnormal fear of glass.

cynophobia   an intense dread of dogs.

deipnophobia   an abnormal fear of dining and dinner conversation.

demonophobia   an abnormal fear of spirits.

demophobia   an intense dislike of crowds.

dermatophobia   an abnormal fear of skin disease. Also called **dermatosiophobia, dermatopathophobia.**

diabetophobia   an intense fear of diabetes.

dinophobia   an abnormal fear of whirlpools.

diplopiaphobia   an abnormal fear of double vision.

dromophobia   an abnormal fear of crossing streets.

dysmorphophobia   an abnormal dread of deformity, usu. in others.

ecophobia, oecophobia, oikophobia   **1.** an abnormal fear of home surroundings.

2. an aversion to home life.

eisoptrophobia, isopterophobia   an abnormal fear of termites.

electrophobia   an abnormal fear of electricity.

emetophobia   an abnormal fear of vomiting.

entomophobia   an abnormal fear of insects.

eosophobia   an abnormal fear of the dawn.

eremiophobia, eremophobia   autophobia.

ergasiophobia   an abnormal fear of work.

ergophobia   a hatred of work.

erotophobia   an abnormal fear of sexual feelings and their physical expression. Also called **miserotica**.

erythrophobia   1. an abnormal fear of the color red.
   2. an abnormal fear of blushing.

eurotophobia   an abnormal fear of female genitals.

febriphobia   an abnormal fear of fever.

felinophobia   ailurophobia.

Francophobia, Gallophobia   an abnormal fear of France or things French.

galeophobia   an abnormal fear of sharks.

gamophobia   an abnormal fear of marriage.

gatophobia   ailurophobia.

genophobia   coitophobia.

gephyrophobia   an abnormal fear of crossing a bridge.

gerascophobia   an abnormal fear of growing old.

Germanophobia   an abnormal fear of Germany, its people, or its culture. Also called **Teutophobia, Teutonophobia.**

geumophobia   an abnormal fear of tastes or flavors.

glossophobia   an abnormal fear of speaking in public or of trying to speak.

graphophobia   a dislike for writing.

gringophobia   in Spain or Latin America, an intense dislike of white strangers.

gymnophobia   an abnormal fear of nudity.

gynephobia, gynophobia   an abnormal fear or hatred of women.

hagiophobia   an intense dislike for saints and the holy.

hamartophobia   an abnormal fear of error or sin.

hedonophobia   an abnormal fear of pleasure.

heliophobia   1. an abnormal sensitivity to the effects of sunlight.
2. an abnormal fear of sunlight.

helminthophobia   an abnormal fear of being infested with worms.

hemophobia   an abnormal fear of blood.

herpetophobia   an abnormal fear of reptiles. Also called **ophidiophobia.**

hierophobia   an abnormal fear of sacred objects.

hippophobia   an abnormal fear of horses.

homilophobia   a hatred for sermons.

hyalophobia   crystallophobia.

hydrophobia   1. an abnormal fear of water.
2. the occurrence in humans of rabies.

hydrophobophobia   an abnormal fear of rabies.

hygrophobia   an abnormal fear of liquids in any form, esp. wine and water.

hylephobia   an intense dislike for wood.

hypengyophobia   an abnormal fear of responsibility.

hypnophobia   an abnormal fear of sleep.

hypsiphobia, hypsophobia, hyposophobia   an abnormal fear of high places.

iatrophobia   an abnormal fear of going to the doctor.

ichthyophobia   an abnormal fear of fish.

iophobia   an abnormal fear of poisons.

kakorrhaphiophobia   an abnormal fear of failure or defeat.

keraunophobia, ceraunophobia   an abnormal fear of thunder and lightning.

kleptophobia, cleptophobia   an abnormal fear of thieves or loss through thievery.

kopophobia   an abnormal fear of mental or physical examination.

kynophobia, cynophobia an abnormal fear of pseudorabies.

laliophobia, lalophobia an abnormal fear of talking.

lepraphobia an abnormal fear of leprosy.

levophobia an abnormal fear of objects on the left side of the body.

meningitophobia an abnormal fear of meningitis.

merinthophobia an abnormal fear of being bound.

metallophobia an abnormal fear of metals.

meteorophobia an abnormal fear of meteors or meteorites.

misophobia, musophobia, mysophobia an abnormal fear of dirt, esp. of being contaminated by dirt.

molysomophobia an abnormal fear of infection.

monopathophobia an abnormal fear of sickness in a specified part of the body.

motorphobia an abnormal fear or dislike of motor vehicles.

musicophobia an intense dislike of music.

musophobia, mysophobia misophobia.

necrophobia 1. an abnormal fear of death.

2. an abnormal fear of corpses.

noctiphobia an abnormal fear of the night.

nosophobia an abnormal fear of contracting disease.

nudophobia, nudiphobia an abnormal fear of nakedness.

nyctophobia an abnormal fear of darkness or night.

ochlophobia   an abnormal fear of crowds.

odontophobia   an abnormal fear of teeth, especially those of animals.

odynophobia   an abnormal fear of pain.

oenophobia, oinophobia   a dislike of or hatred for wine.

olfactophobia   an abnormal fear of smells. Also called **osmophobia**.

ombrophobia   an abnormal fear of rain.

ommatophobia   an abnormal fear of eyes.

onomatophobia   an abnormal fear of a certain name.

ophidiophobia   herpetophobia. Also called **ophiophobia**.

osmophobia   an abnormal fear of odors.

osphresiophobia   an abnormal dislike of odors.

panophobia   **1.** a nonspecific fear; a state of general anxiety. **2.** an abnormal fear of everything. Also called **panphobia, pantaphobia, pantophobia.**

papaphobia   an intense fear or dread of the pope or the papacy.

paralipophobia   an abnormal fear of neglect of some duty.

paraphobia   an abnormal fear of sexual perversion.

parasitophobia   an abnormal fear of parasites.

parthenophobia   an extreme aversion to young girls.

pathophobia   an abnormal fear of disease.

peccatiphobia, peccatophobia   an abnormal fear of sinning.

pediculophobia   an abnormal fear of lice.

pedophobia, paedophobia   an abnormal fear of dolls.

pellagraphobia   an abnormal fear of catching pellagra.

peniaphobia   an abnormal fear of poverty.

phagophobia   an abnormal fear of eating.

pharmacophobia   an abnormal fear of drugs.

phengophobia   an abnormal fear of daylight.

philosophobia   an abnormal fear of philosophy or philosophers.

phobophobia   an abnormal fear of fearing.

phonophobia   an abnormal fear of noise.

photangiophobia   an abnormal fear of photalgia, pain in the eyes caused by light.

photophobia   **1.** an abnormal fear of light.
  2. a painful sensitivity to light, esp. visually. Also called **photodysphoria**.
  3. a tendency to thrive in reduced light, as certain plants.
phthiriophobia   pediculophobia.
phthisiophobia   an abnormal fear of tuberculosis. Also called **tuberculophobia**.
pnigophobia   an abnormal fear of choking.
politicophobia   a dislike or fear of politicians.
polyphobia   an abnormal fear of many things.
ponophobia   an abnormal fear of fatigue, esp. through overworking.
potamophobia   a morbid fear of rivers.
proctophobia   *Med.* a mental apprehension in patients with a rectal disease.
proteinphobia   a strong aversion to protein foods.
psychophobia   an abnormal fear of the mind.
psychrophobia   an abnormal fear of cold temperatures.
pyrexiophobia   an abnormal fear of fever.
pyrophobia   an abnormal fear of fire.
rhabdophobia   an abnormal fear of being beaten.
rhypophobia   an abnormal fear of filth.
Russophobia   an excessive fear or dislike of Russians.

Satanophobia   an excessive fear of Satan.

scabiophobia   an abnormal fear of scabies.

scatophobia   1. coprophobia.

2. an abnormal dread of using obscene language.

scoleciphobia   an abnormal fear of worms. Also called **vermiphobia**.

scopophobia   an abnormal fear of being looked at. Also called **scoptophobia**.

scotophobia   an abnormal fear of the dark.

siderodromophobia   an abnormal fear of railroads or of traveling on trains.

siderophobia   an abnormal fear of the stars.

sitophobia, sitiophobia.   cibophobia.

spectrophobia   an abnormal fear of specters or phantoms.

stasibasiphobia   1. an abnormal conviction that one cannot stand or walk.

2. an abnormal fear of attempting to do either.

syphiliphobia, syphilophobia   an abnormal fear of becoming infected with syphilis.

tabophobia   an abnormal fear of a wasting sickness.

tapinophobia   an abnormal fear of small things.

teleophobia   a dislike and rejection of teleology.

telephonophobia   an abnormal fear of using the telephone.

teratophobia   an abnormal fear of monsters or giving birth to a monster.

Teutophobia, Teutonophobia   Germanophobia.

thalassophobia   an abnormal fear of the sea.

theatrophobia   an abnormal fear of theaters.

theophobia   an abnormal fear of God.

thermophobia   an abnormal fear of heat.

tomophobia   an abnormal fear of surgical operations.

tonitrophobia, tonitruphobia   an abnormal fear of thunder.

topophobia   *Rare.* an abnormal fear of certain places.

toxiphobia, toxicophobia   an abnormal fear of poisoning.

traumatophobia   an excessive or disabling fear of war or physical injury.

tremophobia   an abnormal fear of trembling.

trichinophobia   an abnormal fear of trichinosis. Also called **trichophobia, trichopathophobia.**

tridecaphobia   an abnormal fear of the number 13. Also called **triskaidekaphobia.**

tuberculophobia   phthisiophobia.

tyrannophobia   an intense fear or hatred of tyrants.

uranophobia   an abnormal fear of homosexuals and homosexuality.

urophobia   an abnormal fear of passing urine.

vaccinophobia   an abnormal fear of vaccines and vaccination.

vermiphobia   scoleciphobia.

xenophobia   an abnormal fear or hatred of foreigners and strange things.

xerophobia   an abnormal fear of dryness and dry places, like deserts.

ThE Look and Taste of FeaR

It's true, it's true: fear has a
flavor, like Indian-head pennies.
And another thing: you can
hear your own heart pounding.
It sounds like kids drumming
on empty trash cans.

JERRY DENNIS

Fear is accompanied by a
characteristic odor, a phero-
mone, easily recognized by
others. Often, as soon as they
sense you're afraid, your friends
and relatives run away—useful
for them, but not very helpful
for you.

CARL SAGAN AND ANN DRUYAN

It [death] is like a fever, a physical feeling of dread, a sensation I can only describe by saying that the soul becomes separated from the body.

LEO TOLSTOY

Fear at my heart, as at a cup
My life-blood seemed to sip.

SAMUEL TAYLOR COLERIDGE

It is curious whom fear takes and whom it leaves. . . .
For them [the Mediterranean people] it is a disease, a disturbance as physiological as, say, a toothache to which you give in unresistingly. They feel no more shame in confessing it than to any other physical fact.

BERNARD BERENSON

A thing may be gruesome or dangerous yet you know you can deal with it as your heart has not yet reacted to it; but when your heart reacts you get into panic, the real fear, for that takes the ground from under your feet. You feel that you are gone, demoralized, you suffocate.

CARL JUNG

Spiritual liberation has its sensual component, just as claustrophobia of the soul has its physical symbolism and physiological ground.

DAG HAMMARSKJÖLD

. . . I ordered gin and vermouth; it was brought to me as we pulled out of the station. The knives and forks set up their regular jingle; the bright landscape rolled past the windows. But I had no mind for these smooth things; instead, fear worked like yeast in my thoughts, and the fermentation brought to the surface, in great gobs of scum, the images of disaster: a loaded gun held carelessly at a stile, a horse rearing and rolling over, a shaded pool with a submerged stake, an elm bough falling

suddenly on a still morning, a car at a blind corner; all the
catalogue of threats to civilized life rose and haunted me; I even
pictured a homicidal maniac mouthing in the shadows swinging
a length of lead pipe.

Evelyn Waugh

While transferring the fruit from the can to the sterile plate,
be very sure that no part of the body, including the hands, be
directly over the can or the plate at any time. If possible,
keep the head, upper part of the body, arms, etc. at least one
foot away.

Howard Hughes

Chlorine is my madeline. Its smell, like Proust's famous taste of
cookie, express-mails me back to childhood, calling up my fear
and longing with a swift and startling intensity.

Lesley Dornen

I was in an elevator several years ago, riding up to see my dentist. I inhaled some perfume and became very claustrophobic and full of fear—like, *immediately*, just overwhelmed with fear. A few seconds later, I realized it was the same perfume that my stepmother used to wear.

HENRY ROLLINS

I have awakened in the night, being slightly unwell and felt so much afraid. The sensation of fear is accompanied by troubled beating of heart, sweat, trembling of muscles. . . .

CHARLES DARWIN

It is always night and I always
escape through an exploding
maelstrom of fire. The land of
my dreams is fraught with
anxiety. My house is a
desolate shell.

KEN RUSSELL

When I was about seven, I
dreamt I was walking through a
corridor in a hospital, and there
was a stretcher with a body all
covered up. As I walked past, it
popped up, and it was David
Bowie with, you know, those
eyes, and then it chased me
around the hospital. That's
stuck with me ever since.

ANDREA LEWIS

God forbid that my worst enemy should ever have the Nights
and the Sleeps that I have had, night after night. Surprised by
Sleep, while I struggled to remain awake, starting up to bless my
own loud Screams that had awakened me.

SAMUEL TAYLOR COLERIDGE

I have no fear of God, and yet fear keeps me awake at night, fear of the devil. And if I believe in the devil, I must believe in God. And if evil is abhorrent to me, I must be a saint.

ANAÏS NIN

Fear tastes like a rusty knife and do not let her into your house.

JOHN CHEEVER

Ourselves and Others

We are afraid of truth, afraid of fortune, afraid of death, and afraid of each other.

RALPH WALDO EMERSON

My biggest fear is losing contact with other people, forgetting how to express things, or just suddenly not being able to communicate at all.

LAURIE ANDERSON

I have a horror for all rhetoric and romanticism and that verbal
effort of the mind to try to "add an inch to one's height."

ANDRÉ GIDE

One dreads the loss of all things, all people close and dear.
There is an acute fear of abandonment. Being alone in the
house, even for a moment, causes me an exquisite panic
and trepidation.

WILLIAM STYRON

There is undoubtedly in our society, and in all societies I
imagine, but with different forms and rhythms, a profound
logophobia, a sort of dumb fear of . . . the great, incessant, and
disorderly buzzing of discourse.

MICHEL FOUCAULT

Eventually . . . I would become so exhausted that I would just throw myself on the bed or on the floor until they came back. Every day was a nightmare, because I was afraid that they would leave me when it turned dark. I had an intense fear of being abandoned, and I remember practically all of my childhood as being lived in a state of constant tension and fear.

TRUMAN CAPOTE

Everything has to be right. At home, I have to know that my little boy isn't going to barge in, and be reasonably sure the doorbell won't ring. I can never make a call in front of anyone.

At school, if I have a free period and five calls to make, first I have to find an office that's not occupied. Even though I'm panicked and flustered, my face is turning red, my palms are sweating, and my voice sounds like Minnie Mouse, I manage to get one call made. Then someone walks in and I lose my space. I end up walking the halls looking for another private place to call from until my free period is over.

ADRIENNE
PHOBIA PATIENT

Solitude scares me. It makes me think about love, death, and war. I need distraction from anxious black thoughts.

BRIGITTE BARDOT

Climbing the stairs [of school] in this fashion with nothing before me but boots and calves and scraping of hundreds of feet in my ears, I was often seized—I seem to remember—by my revulsion at being hemmed in by this multitude. . . . The corridors and classrooms that finally came into view, are among the horrors that have embedded themselves . . . in my dreams.

WALTER BENJAMIN

But most of all, the thing that I find frightening is vibrations in houses. It can even be outside—I've felt it outside. It is a feeling that something is wrong, that something is *here*, and that frightens me a lot.

MICHAEL MCDOWELL

. . . I remember her [the principal] trying to touch me and I—I pulled back. I pulled back from anybody who wanted to touch me—anybody.

JACK LEMMON

During my childhood in Budapest, I always had the feeling that someone was watching. That's the secret of the police state: you never know whether your friend, colleague, or classmate is an informer. You tailor your movements accordingly.

KATI MARTIN

In the five years that I had lived in New York I had never thought about anyone coming through the windows, but now the fear was so real that I checked each one of the eight windows to be sure they were locked. That didn't help. The longer I thought about the windows and the fact that it was getting dark, the more nervous I got. I switched on all the lights and turned on the radio.

HOPE LAMBERT

Sometimes the objects of my fear change, and sometimes the quality of my fear changes—but I find too much fear, in a way.

I can't go to sleep in a hotel without thinking, "Who is in the room underneath me, dead drunk and smoking a cigarette and about to fall asleep so that the room catches fire? When was the last time that they changed the batteries in the smoke detector?"

STEPHEN KING

I just feel safer being in San Francisco. Here [in L.A.], it's like being a hemophiliac in a razor factory.

ROBIN WILLIAMS

But I like to explore the ugly sides of human nature, as well as the beautiful sides. I don't want to be afraid.

PATRICIA ARQUETTE

The emotions in his [John Lennon's] music were the emotions I could never express .... Those were the feelings that I had to bury inside myself, that I could never let out for fear they would be just so horrendous. Those feelings that, when they finally did come out, it was out of the barrel of a gun.

MARK DAVID CHAPMAN

I suppose one of the reasons why I grew up feeling the need to cause laughter was the perpetual fear of being its unwitting object.

CLIVE JAMES

Our whole education is just one long humiliation, and it was
even more so when I was a child. One of the wounds that I've
found hardest to bear in my adult life has been the fear of
humiliation, and the sense of being humiliated. Every time I
read a review, for instance—whether laudatory or not—this
feeling awakes.

INGMAR BERGMAN

Each man is afraid of his neighbor's disapproval—a thing which
to the great run of the human race is more dreaded than wolves
and death.

MARK TWAIN

It was the summer of fear, for Frankie. . . . This August she was
twelve and five-sixth years old. She was five feet and three-
quarter inches tall. . . . In the past year she had grown four
inches. . . . If she reached her height on her eighteenth birthday
. . . she would grow to be over nine feet tall. . . . She would be
a freak.

CARSON MCCULLERS

When I understood what these men actually *did*, I was horrified. For an Irish Catholic kid in those years, sex itself was terrifying enough; the homosexual variety seemed proof of the existence of Satan. Gradually the stereotypes I carried were broken by experience and knowledge. At the same time I was roaming around as a reporter seeing riots and wars, too much poverty and too many dead bodies. The ambiguities, masks, and games of human sexuality seemed a minor issue compared with the horrors of the wider world.

PETE HAMIL

Homophobia in those who cultivate it when they ought to know better is a moral failing.

JOAN WAITKEVICZ

Fear of sexuality is the new disease. . . . Cancerphobia taught us
the fear of a polluting environment; now we have the fear of
polluting people that AIDS anxiety inevitably communicates.
Fear of the communion cup, fear of surgery, fear of
contaminated blood, whether Christ's blood or your neighbor's.
Life—blood, sexual fluids—is the bearer of contamination,
these fluids are potentially lethal.

SUSAN SONTAG

"My father believes," said Kyo slowly, "that the essence of man
is anguish, the consciousness of his own fatality, from which all
fears are born, even the fear of death. . . . One can always find
terror in himself. One only needs to look deep enough:
fortunately one can act.

ANDRÉ MALRAUX

Long before the eventual
mutilation, woman is haunted
by the horror of growing old....
What is to become of her when
she no longer has any hold on
him? This is what she anxiously
asks herself while
she helplessly looks on the
degradation of this fleshly
object which she identifies
with herself.

SIMONE DE BEAUVOIR

Amazing how truly aging is a
process of horror and dis-
illusioning to me. However
mad I was, I never dreamed it
would be like this.

ALLEN GINSBERG

. . . the biggest difference between my life before and after baldness is that now people fear me.

RICHARD BROOKHISER

Man justifiably fears being devoured by woman, who is nature's proxy.

CAMILLE PAGLIA

Falling in love terrifies me. It's the most dangerous thing we do.

JAN REYNOLDS

The realization hit me heavily like a .44 Magnum smashing into my skull. My heart started beating with a quick dread, and my blood froze in my veins. My stomach did backflips; I had to race to the bathroom to avoid a major incident. The ordeal I was about to face is one of the most grisly, macabre, and chilling experiences known to a woman.

Dating. I will have to start dating again.

CYNTHIA HEIMEL

The idea of dating is frightening. You worry about so many things—not just AIDS. Also serial killers.

22-YEAR-OLD POLICE REPORTER

I always weep at weddings—weep for the sheer terror that it might be mine.

MARGARET MITCHELL

The dread of loneliness is greater than the fear of bondage, so we get married.

CYRIL CONNOLLY

It all gets down to love and fear of losing love.

JEFF BRIDGES

. . . she will grow very silent and watch me, study me as I move about, and never ask what is torturing me, never, never, because that is the one thing she fears, the one thing she dreads to know. *I don't love you!* Can't she hear me screaming it? *I don't love you!* Over and over I yell it, with lips tight, with hatred in my heart, with despair, with hopeless rage. But the words never leave my lips. I look at her and I am tongue-tied. I can't do it. . . .

HENRY MILLER

If the slightest formality attaches to any social occasion, I avoid it like the plague. I'm deathly afraid of everything that seems obligatory or compulsory, no matter whether it's a party, club, family visit, or friendship. Fickh is the only friend I have, and I've always been frightened of him.

HERMAN HESSE

The fear [phrenophobia—the fear of going crazy] is totally groundless because nervous breakdowns don't exist. What does exist is the possibility of exaggerated expression of the four basic emotions—mad, glad, sad, and scared.

GARY EMERY

Nathan. Nathan. I was afraid of you then. I am afraid now. I have been afraid of all manner of things every moment I have spent on this planet, on this monstrous, beautiful, terrifying planet with all its strange creatures and its abundant water, and all of its human people. I am afraid now. I will be afraid to die here.

WALTER TEVIS

I think the main problem of living that we are now faced with is how to maintain an identity in a super state. A vast agoraphobia may be one of the neuroses of the next century—too many people. A feeling of, "My God, I'm getting lost, I'm going to drown in them. Stop, stop, no more!"

GORE VIDAL

Like most guys, I break out in a cold sweat at the mere sight of a dressing room. I break down at the thought of a sale-crazed mob.

J.D. POLLACK

To fear a crowd and yet fear solitude, to fear to go unguarded, to fear the very guards themselves, to be unwilling to dispense with an armed escort and yet to feel displeasure at the sight of one's attendants carrying arms: what a hateful predicament.

XENOPHON

The New and the Unknown

Everybody is afraid of anything they don't know anything about.

JIMI HENDRIX

There was a quiet buzz . . . we were being extremely well-bred, all of us, for the party . . . and I know now that I was not the only Westerner who was scared shaky at the immediate prospect of eating her first raw oyster, and was putting it off for as long as possible.

M.F.K. FISHER

I had horrible teeth, so my parents used to take me to an Italian dentist who had a unique piece of equipment—a cross between a chainsaw and a sewing machine. He'd stick this thing in my mouth and it would go voodn-voodn-voodn-voooodnnnnn—no novocaine. I learned to dread the sound of the word dentist.

FRANK ZAPPA

The world fears new experience more than it fears anything.

D.H. LAWRENCE

I've known fear since my childhood. . . . I myself hate suspense and that's why I would never allow anyone to make a soufflé at my home; my oven has no glass door! We'd have to wait 40 minutes to find out if the soufflé turned out right and that is more than I can stand!

ALFRED HITCHCOCK

My [grandmother] . . . lived the latter years of her life in the horrible suspicion that electricity was dripping invisibly all over the house . . . out of empty sockets if the wall switch had been left on. Nothing could ever clear this up for her.

JAMES THURBER

. . . going into the subway, I felt I was really going down into hell. As I went down the steps—going deeper into it—I realized it was almost as difficult to back up and get out of it than to go through with this ride. It was the total fear of the unknown: the wind from the train, the sounds, the smells, and the different lights and the mood of that was really special in a traumatic way.

DAVID LYNCH

. . . fear is a synthetic apprehension of the transcendent as dreadful.

JEAN PAUL SARTRE

Once when I was a child, I looked out into the hall and such a feeling of fear and despair came over me, for no untoward reason, that I burst into tears. I was looking into the future, and what I saw has not yet been realized. I can only wait for it to happen. Is it some ghastly occurrence or simply deterioration and failure and final loneliness? . . . I don't know, but I feel trapped and doomed.

WILLIAM S. BURROUGHS

The one permanent emotion of the inferior man is fear—fear of the unknown, the complex, the inexplicable. What he wants beyond everything else is safety.

H.L. MENCKEN

There are a number of reasons why people might suffer from technophobia—that is a morbid fear of technological advance. . . . It is the fear of re-education. . . . It is not pleasant to begin a process you had thought was over and done forever, and to abandon a superiority that had been painfully achieved.

ISAAC ASIMOV

. . . learning is never what one expects. Every step of learning is a new task and the fear the man is experiencing begins to mount mercilessly, unyieldingly. His purpose becomes a battlefield. And thus he has stumbled upon the first of his natural enemies: fear! A terrible enemy—treacherous and difficult to overcome. It remains concealed at every turn of the way, prowling, waiting. And if the man, terrified in its presence, runs away, his enemy will have put an end to his quest.

CARLOS CASTANEDA

Do American faces so often look so lost because they are most tragically trapped between a very real dread of coming alive to something more than merely existing, and an equal dread of going down to the grave without having done more than merely to be comfortable?

If so, this is truly the American disease.

NELSON ALGREN

When you can't see what's coming at you, that produces fear. We just don't know how to handle it, don't know how to deal with it.

GERRY COONEY

Rubashov had been beaten up repeatedly during his last imprisonment. . . . He had learned that every *known* physical pain was bearable; if one knew beforehand exactly what was going to happen to one, one stood it as a surgical operation—for instance, the extraction of a tooth. Really bad was only the unknown, which gave one no chance to foresee one's reactions and no scale to calculate one's capacity of resistance. And the worst was the fear that one would do or say something which could not be recalled.

ARTHUR KOESTLER

What upsets me is not knowing what to expect, the sensation that something unknown to me is hanging over my head or being hatched against me behind my back. This makes me nervous and inattentive; I imagine catastrophes and can't think sensibly or deal with anything except my own uncertainty. This psychophysical uncertainty grows to become fear of the potential and unknown threat, of not being prepared for it, able to stand up to it, or even making matters worse by doing something inappropriate. Sometimes, the fear can become a general existential anxiety. . . . That is, I fear the decisions other people make less than the decisions I might be expected to make myself.

VACLAV HAVEL

She [my wife] was afraid of anything unknown, of the jungle or the mountains. . . . Nature in general horrified her. Her idea of a beautiful landscape was a meadow with cows grazing, no mountains in the distance, nothing else. The sea or storms frightened her. She'd say, "Yes, yes, they're beautiful, but it's terrible. I don't want to look at it, thank you. Let's go inside. It's almost the cocktail hour." What was unknown, overpowering, not within human measure, geysers, tornadoes, thunderstorms, she hated.

PAUL BOWLES

All of my fears and cares are of this world; if there is another, an honest man has nothing to fear from it.

ROBERT BURNS

Taking a new step, uttering a new word is what people fear the most.

FYODOR DOSTOYEVSKY

Open and Closed

First of all, I couldn't find the attic in Mia's house. I mean I have never been in an attic. I'm a famous claustrophobic; wild horses couldn't get me into an attic.

WOODY ALLEN

Even though I'm cooped up in a train, it's not like in a plane. . . . Now that I think about it, I've realized that I've had a few claustrophobic tendencies ever since I was a kid. At dinner, I had to sit at one end of the table or the other, not in the middle. At a movie, I always sat on the aisle. In an elevator, I'm always uneasy.

JOHN MADDEN

I completely lost control. Everything closed in on me. I couldn't breathe. . . . Here I was a professional athlete, unafraid of physical punishment and yet I couldn't control this fear [claustrophobia]. Compared to catching a ball with a linebacker staring you in the face, it seems minor. But I couldn't control it.

RICK MASSIE

I can't stand nobody touching my toes. I have a real phobia about it. Like at night when I sleep I have to have my toes sticking out from the sheet. I can't have them covered. That drives me berserk.

ROSEANNE ARNOLD

I don't mind elevators—if they're glass—but it's being closed up that I fear. I get the feeling that I am in an upright coffin set on end if I can't see out. It's terrible.

MAYA ANGELOU

The varieties of hilarious torture were infinite. One of the most successful played on my suffocation phobia: I was locked in the map closet. This space was about eighteen inches wide and perhaps ten inches deep—a perfect vertical tomb. . . .The closet door opened from the outside only. How well I knew. Once I was buried alive, my resultant panic—rather like dropping a match into a box of fireworks—was everything my tormentors could hope for. Terrified, screaming in the dark, I would try to kick the door down.

HUME CRONYN

To say that I had been terrified and was still terrified would be too much of an everyday statement. No, I had been struck with a foreignness, I had taken a deep breath of unsupportable air. I was not at all myself, and my new loathing that was so much more than a fear of the ship was in itself an illness.

DORIS LESSING

Claustrophobia relates to death. A closed-in feeling relates to smothering. Fear of heights suggests falling in a way that relates to death as does tightness in the chest and stomach. The fear of the unknown may be a fear of death. What will happen if I get on? Will I die? Will the plane crash? These things flood through their minds.

T.W. CUMMINGS
FORMER PILOT AND DIRECTOR OF FREEDOM FROM FEAR OF FLYING, INC.

An hour later, after crawling home on the small back streets, I made what I thought was a logical decision: something about freeways was scaring me, so I would just stop driving on them. It would be a little extra trouble but it would solve my problem.

It didn't. . . . Pretty soon, I wasn't traveling by car, I wasn't walking; I wasn't, in fact, doing much of anything. Each time I left the house I got scared; is it going to happen again? Where?

JANE GASSNER PATRICK

One woman I know has a phobia that began when she witnessed a traffic accident. . . . She began to have the feeling that something like that could happen to her, and she found herself getting uptight when she drove. Her heart would pound, she felt lightheaded, her hands felt numb, breathing was difficult, and she was afraid she would lose control of the car, maybe go off a bridge. Almost as bad, she feared that if she stopped, someone might ram into her car so she began to be terrified of any driving.

MANUEL ZANE

I start a little walk down the street. About one hundred feet from the house, I am compelled to rush back in horror of being so far away . . . one hundred feet away . . . from home and security.

At times this emotional effect remains merely a diffuse state of terror, an intensity running the whole scale from vague anxiety to the intensest feeling of impending death. . . . I am in terror of the seizure of terror and I fear seizure at a given distance.

WILLIAM ELLERY LEONARD

Being run by fear is the worst thing anyone can do to themselves. If you're afraid to come out of your house because you're afraid of walking the streets, you're assigning yourself to some kind of purgatory. It's not quite hell, but it might as well be.

KEITH RICHARDS

There it was, the old fear, back again, whenever I had to go someplace. And I was, at this point, afraid of my fear. My anxiety attacks had become so intense that I was often immobilized, paralyzed. So I hadn't dashed very far when the terror, greater than yesterday's, less than tomorrow's, swallowed me up like a vacuum cleaner.

BARBARA GORDON

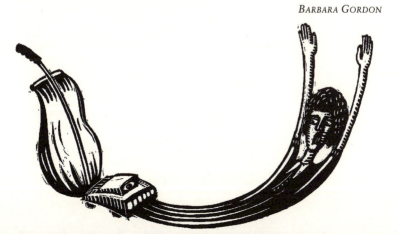

Suddenly, and for no apparent reason, my body went berserk. At first I thought I was going to throw up, but before I could even think what to do about that, a host of other horrifying sensations began to surface. I became hot and sweaty, although I was shaking as if cold. My vision blurred and my feet went so numb that I honestly couldn't believe that I could brake to stop the car. I felt totally out of control of myself and my body. I ended becoming hysterical.

ANONYMOUS PHOBIA PATIENT

I did all my Christmas shopping through a catalog, I became obsessed with fear. I was afraid that the apartment was going to catch fire, so I began sleeping on the couch. We had two cars, but no matter which one I was riding in, I thought it was going to explode.

SANDRA LEFFLER

"As I explained to Mr. DuPont at our first game, I suffer from an obscure complaint, agoraphobia, the fear of open spaces. I cannot bear the open horizon. I must sit and face the hotel." The deal continued.

"Oh I'm sorry," Bond's voice was grave, interested. "That's a very rare disability. I've always been able to understand claustrophobia but not the other way around. How did it come about?"

Goldfinger picked up his cards and began to arrange his hand. "I have no idea," he said equably.

IAN FLEMING

I was afraid I would embarrass myself in public, lose control, or pass out. I even had trouble going to church: I volunteered as an usher because that way I could always stand in the back.

ANONYMOUS PHOBIA PATIENT

When we went to church I always picked an aisle seat as close to the door as possible so that I could escape if I had to. Usually I would just sweat and white knuckle it. I always left the church mentally and physically drawn. It ruined every Sunday.

Restaurants were the same way. When we went out, I always made a lot of trips to the bathroom because I thought I might get sick and pass out, which I never did.

Passing out is what a lot of phobics are afraid of but it never happens.

WANDA FALCI

Even the thought of a wedding—every other young woman's dream—terrified me. We were married by a judge. At my fiancé's insistence eight members of our families attended the ceremony, but there was no reception—I couldn't have faced one. Immediately after we left on our honeymoon.

We planned a two-week motor trip through New England, an area I knew and loved. It lasted one week. Then all of my fears overwhelmed me and we returned.

MARGO BLOCK

High And Low

Ten, that was the magic number. When friends who lived on higher floors would invite me over for dinner, I'd say "Why don't you come over to my place?" I became a very good cook.

JERILYN ROSS

Social relationships have also presented their difficulties. I try very hard not to like any man who lives above the fourth floor. A phrase that can make me fall in love is "Want to come and see my basement apartment?"

SUSAN BERMAN

Just the mention of a hotel makes me turn cold. When I'm in a hotel room, I worry about getting so depressed I might jump out of a window.

CHARLES SCHULZ

I've always had a healthy fear of heights, and it's difficult for me to even watch window washers or people bungee jumping. My heart instinctively beats faster, and my palms gush with sweat.

ELENA BUCCIARELLI

I looked over the edge and was overcome by dizziness: I could never climb back down. I would lose my grip, fall, and die. But the way to the top was even worse; steeper and more treacherous. I heard more sobbing; I wondered who it was and realized that it was me.

Time passed and dusk began to gather. Silent now, I lay on my stomach, stupified by fear and fatigue, unable to move.

MORTON HUNT

As the months went by I commenced having a dread of high hills, especially when the fields consisted of pasture land and were level with the grass clipped short like the grass on a well-kept lawn. I likewise commenced to dread high things. . . . I even had a fear of crowds of people and later wide streets and parks.

I have outgrown the fear of crowds largely but an immense building or a high rocky bluff fills me with dread. Ugly architecture intensifies the fear.

The malady is always present.

VINCENT
PHOBIA PATIENT

We were talking and laughing,
and I had approached and was,
in fact, on the George Washing-
ton Bridge without having
remembered my weakness.
There were no preliminaries
this time. The seizure came with
a rush. The strength went out
of my legs. I gasped for breath
and felt the terrifying loss of
sight. I was, at the same time,
determined to conceal the
symptoms from my daughter.
I made it to the other side of the
bridge, but I was violently
shaken.

JOHN CHEEVER

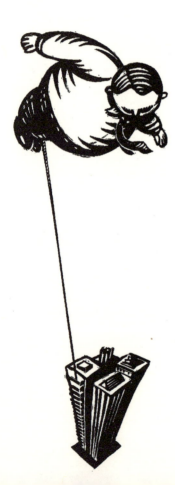

My phobia is high places. As long as I don't look down I can be in any high place, but I can't look down. When I'm in a high place and look down, I become lightheaded and have this floating sensation that if I stepped off a balcony I would float. I have to immediately overcome this sensation and reconcile myself that I do not have the ability to float in air.

FRED WILLIAMSON

I was gradually turning into a habitual sleepwalker, haunting the apartment corridor, staring, fast asleep, into my parents' bedroom. Once I awoke leaning far out the window looking six stories down into the depths of the interior courtyard. As I came awake, the terror of the height whistled up through my veins, a fear I have never lost.

ARTHUR MILLER

I once fell through a window because I was trying to avoid the stairs.

GARY SHAUL

As the plane had taxied to get into position for takeoff, Phil [Spector] freaked out. He was screaming, "I'm not flying on this plane! These people are losers. And the plane's not going to make it."

SONNY BONO

That's what I'm always afraid of. I've always said I would never fly on a plane where the pilot believes in reincarnation.

SPALDING GRAY

After promising myself never again, I made the crazy mistake of taking another nonstop flight across the Atlantic. Trapped between the parentheses of a twelve-hour flight, I lost identity, destiny, and even destination. Besides which, this time the flight was so perfect that for a minute I was sure the plane had stopped in mid-air. I've always been afraid of the plane crashing, but this time I conceived of a new fear: terror that the plane would stay in the air forever.

GABRIEL GARCÍA MÁRQUEZ

As you know I don't fly—haven't for sixteen years—and no assignment, no matter how enticing, will get me aloft again.

GLENN GOULD

My heart started beating fast and I got butterflies. Then it escalated to feeling that things were unreal and I became very focused on sensations in my body, my toes, and tongue and I turned to the man next to me and told him I was having a hard time breathing.

My fear is mainly claustrophobia but after a bumpy flight to Minneapolis last summer I have a fear of crashing, too.

JUDY DEBROEF

Light and Dark

Some of the people are afraid of the dark and some are afraid to leave it.

BEAU MAVERICK

It is impossible to imagine the magnitude of the terror brought by total darkness to people who have never experienced it before—it is a terror that destroys all reason. . . . As the old saying goes "fear peoples the darkness with monsters."

AKIRA KUROSAWA

The core of [my phobia] was an abject fear of light . . . so overpowering that I darted out in the daylight only to be driven back as if by an unseen force into a darkened room where I could find the comparative peace and feeling of safety, although even there I had to fight off periods of intense fear.

ANONYMOUS PHOBIA PATIENT

I have said that I heard screams. (I have since read that screaming, with hysteria, is a common reaction even to expected total eclipses.)

The second before the sun went out we saw a wall of dark shadow come speeding at us. We no sooner saw it than it was upon us, like thunder. It roared up the valley. . . . It was the monstrous swift shadow cone of the moon. . . . We saw the wall of shadow coming and screamed before it hit.

ANNIE DILLARD

As a kid I was afraid of the dark, of letting my hand dangle over the bed and having it grabbed by the bogeyman. Luckily, all it took to calm my racing heart was the sound of my parents' voices downstairs. But the minute I was left alone in the house—when I was too young to go out, but too old for a baby sitter—my imagination ran wild.

AMY SHORT

Did you ever, when abandoned by your nurse to the horrors of a big black bedroom, see a grinning face advance towards you from the distant apex of a huge cone which lay before your closed eyes—advance gradually, but unavoidably, till in spite of your struggles, its monstrous features were so close to yours that you could feel them; then, almost suddenly, start back from you, flit away, diminish till nothing but the dark eyeballs remain in sight, and disappear presently to return with all its terrors?

SIR RICHARD FRANCIS BURTON

. . . not ordinary fear, but a
kind of night sickness—a
spiritual nausea which hung
like a cloud over my life. . . .
My overloaded heart was
bursting with its packed weight
of loneliness and terror; I was
strangling, without speech,
without articulation, in my own
secretions, groping like a blind
sea thing with no eyes and a
thousand feelers toward light,
toward life, toward beauty
and order, out of that hell of
chaos. . . .

THOMAS WOLFE

The ideas of goblins and spirits have really no more to do with darkness than light. Yet let but a foolish maid inculcate these often into the mind of a child and raise them there together, possibly he shall never be able to separate them again as long as he lives; but darkness shall ever afterward bring with it those frightful ideas and they should be joined that he can no more bear the one than the other.

JOHN LOCKE

When they would send me to the store after dark, boy that was an agonizing couple of blocks. I would usually wind up running like hell for the last block home. I was ashamed of myself. I thought, "My brother isn't afraid of the dark. Is it something I will outgrow or what?"

RONALD REAGAN

I looked over my shoulder. The trees and bushes with the strange noises in them seemed to take on the form of monsters with long arms. I ran to catch up. Then, by the time I had once more looked furtively over my shoulder at the shapeless pursuing forms of the darkness, I discovered that I was behind again. Why did father walk so fast? And so block after block, I alternately lagged behind and ran, fearful of being lost and swallowed up in the night or grabbed by some demon in the dark.

WILLIAM O. DOUGLAS

Fame and Failure

Rahv asked me how I liked
being a success . . . and I started
to shake all over and couldn't
even light a cig.

ANNE SEXTON

So, I have a horror of success.

VINCENT VAN GOGH

My worst enemy is sitting right here at this table. . . . It's me. . . . I'm the only one I really have to fear. I can't accept success. Right on the brink of success, something within me says that I don't deserve it, and I snatch it away from myself by committing crimes. . . . I have a compulsion to destroy myself.

DAVID BEGELMAN

Once a climber presses the face [of a rock], a fearful cycle begins. It is an unnoticed welling up of animal fear that first makes him hug the rock; hugging weakens his footholds and blinds him to purchases that might be within grasp; and this, now real, danger feeds the original fear.

TREVANIAN

. . .we seem to brood so incessantly on our weaknesses, we seem to have so many phobias; like everybody who really cares about rock, we spend so much time worrying how many more years.

PETE TOWNSHEND

Our best-selling book on phobias is lacking an author cover photo because—you guessed it—the author has a phobia about having his picture taken.

BARBARA QUICK

It rubs me the wrong way, a camera. It doesn't matter who it is, someone in my family could be pointing a camera around. It's a frightening feeling. . . . Cameras make ghosts out of people.

BOB DYLAN

I had a recurring nightmare: coming to Yankee Stadium in a cab, wearing my uniform, trying to crawl through a hole. I can see Whitey and Billy and Casey and my other teammates. I'm supposed to be with them but I can't squeeze through the hole in the wall. I'm stuck. I hear the public address speaker blare out my name: "At bat . . . number seven . . . Mickey Mantle. . ." That's when I'd wake up, drenched in sweat.

MICKEY MANTLE

My greatest fear is poverty. That scares the heck out of me.

DICK GREGORY

I'm scared to death of being poor. It's like a fat girl who loses 500 pounds but is always fat inside. I grew up poor and will always feel poor inside.

CHER

I wake up in a cold sweat
during the night, every night,
and think about some girl
sleeping in a bed with Brandon
Walsh pillowcases and her
boyfriend coming over in
Brandon Walsh boxer shorts.
It's like a nightmare. It's turning
into a runaway train, and
there's nothing that can stop it.

JASON PRIESTLY

The first element is the mystery,
the fact that you don't know
where the writing comes from.
The fear is "What happens if it
all dries up?"

NORMAN MAILER

Of course you run out, maybe not indefinitely, but everybody runs out of some material for a while. And it's a very frightening experience. It's an awesome thing to think "Oh my God, that's the only thing that's ever supplied me with any success or made us any money."

BRIAN WILSON

I live in horror that I won't know when to quit. I don't want to be one of those writers who run out of things to write and then go around the rest of their lives talking about writing but not really producing anything anyone wants to read.

ELLEN GILCHRIST

One of the things many of us are afraid to do is admit we're scared. That can leave us sitting at our typewriters and whistling in the dark, and it's tough to get much accomplished that way.

LAWRENCE BLOCK

When I was a child I lived in dread of having to sing in public. This was a common forfeit in party games, but I would do anything else humiliating in preference.

SIMON FRITH

Oh, if only I were not afraid of painting! But, in the end, I want each brush stroke to achieve the absolute and give the perfect image of the testicles of the painting, testicles that are not mine.

SALVADOR DALI

I was terrified most of the time.

DIANE ARBUS

At first I was scared to death. I had butterflies in my stomach—
to this day I still get a little nervous before giving a speech.

LEE IACOCCA

At gym class when Mr. D. would call attendance, I would be
overcome with fear. Suppose I didn't answer "here. . .?"
Suppose that at that moment I was unable to speak, temporarily
struck mute? Suppose instead of responding in an appropriate
manner I swore involuntarily? And what if I did not recognize
my own name? What if I opened my mouth and a pigeon
flew out?

DAVID FEINBERG

Any actor who claims he is immune to stage fright is either lying or he is no actor.

OTIS SKINNER

. . . at one point I looked up and saw rows of puzzled people staring down at me.

I remember their silence. I remember the emcee pointing to his watch and waving frantically at me. I remember sweating and thinking how remarkable it was that I was soaking wet on the outside but had not one drop of moisture in my mouth. I remember standing backstage, frozen against a wall for an hour.

DENIS LEARY

I get terrible stage fright . . . when I'm very, very nervous. The last ten minutes before I go on, my hands are really shaking to the point of having trouble working with my makeup or anything. It hits me about fifteen minutes before we go on. I'm almost sick to my stomach and it's difficult for me. It used to be that you'd have a shot of vodka and tonic, and you'd calm down.

STEVIE NICKS

I realized something was seriously wrong with me. I had no control over my breathing. I was hyperventilating. My palms started to sweat and my heart was beating out of my chest. I could speak but I couldn't think straight. I remember I made a joke. Thank God, mine is a buffoon act.

WILLARD SCOTT

Animals

I have a non-negotiable animal phobia. Can't even stand fish in a bowl.

LUTHER VANDROSS

I inherited from my mother a blinding terror of birds and bats. Even today I loathe the touch of feathers.

GRAHAM GREENE

Luposlipaphobia: the fear of being pursued by timberwolves around a kitchen table while wearing socks on a newly waxed floor.

GARY LARSON

In biology class, talking about body parts made me faint.

I think my imagination was too vivid. My Mom and I drove by an auto accident once, and even though I couldn't see the injuries I imagined them and fainted. I couldn't look at any kind of raw meat.

It got so bad that when a teacher handed me back a math test with corrections written in red ink, I thought of blood. The next thing I knew, I was lying on the ground.

17-YEAR-OLD HIGH-SCHOOL STUDENT

Snakes. Anything with a tail that's longer than usual. Rats and mice. Possums are weird. I know they're harmless, but that tail—I still haven't gotten over it. That's really all.

BILL MURRAY

But as of yet I had no need of God. My nightmare world was terrifying enough without him. Snakes persisted.

ANTHONY BURGESS

Sarah and I don't like snakes. I'm not going anywhere near one.

PRINCE ANDREW

"Snakes! Why does it have to be snakes?!"

INDIANA JONES

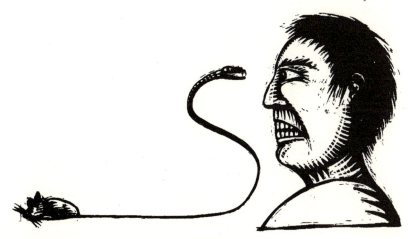

Whether it was the sound of its hissing or the hypnotic glitter of its black lidless eyes that paralyzed me, I'll never know. But for an instant the strength went out of me and I sank into a void of dread. The next instant I had come out of it, striking blindly at the snake as it struck back at the shovel and I could hear its good fang pinging against the blade until it caught him in the middle and chopped him in two. I chopped it into tiny pieces, and then I built a fire and burned it with the nauseating scent adding to my hysteria. And I took Jean into the house and searched it and locked the doors and checked my rifle and took her to bed and didn't get up until the next morning.

CHESTER HIMES

I'm thousands of times more
afraid of chiggers than I am of
mosquitoes. I got my last
chigger bite when I was a boy
in Kansas City. It still itches a
little. . . .Where we live is many
hundreds of miles northeast of
where the most northeasterly
chigger bites have ever been
reported. I avoid the high grass
anyway, just in case.

CALVIN TRILLIN

. . . we have a big orifice that
insects can crawl inside of. . . . I
think I probably had that fear
when I was little. When I was
out in the woods, I'd sit on my
hands to make sure that no
bugs could permeate my
underpants and go up inside my
crotch.

MADONNA

At heart, though, "Do Clams Bite?" is not about events or people. It is about fear. It is about several boyhood fears: the fear of saying the wrong thing, fear of sex, fear of oblivion, fear of becoming like one's parents, fear of other boys (especially those who carry knives), and—most of all—the fear of having a hunk of oneself bitten off by a clam. As a boy, I suffered this fear in silence. Only later did I learn that I had not been the only sufferer. . . . Girls fear for their toes, but in boys this pelecypodophobia centers, as so many boyhood fears do, on the penis.

ERIC KRAFT

Life and Death

It [death] interferes in the end.

SIMONE DE BEAUVOIR

You know that I'm at death's door. But the trouble is that I'm afraid to knock.

SOMERSET MAUGHAM

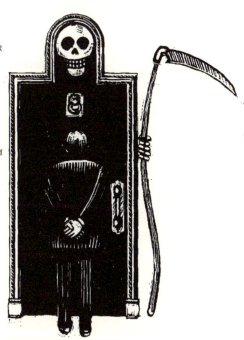

I had a childhood fear that we would all be in our graves, in the darkness, not moving until Judgment Day. That fear has persisted, that there's life in dead bodies, that it's locked in there and can't get out.

ANNE RICE

The dramatic scenes I visualized were terrifying; first the fatal telegram arriving at the house, and my aunt and uncle calling me into the drawing-room to break the news, then the tear-sodden journey in the train. . . .Then, as a fitting climax, I imagined the front bedroom enshrouded in funereal twilight with the blinds down and mother lying still and dead under a sheet, like a waxwork.

NOËL COWARD

Fear is the basis of existence. We have surrounded ourselves with this bright world because of death.

WHITLEY STRIEBER

I ask myself why I am so
frightened of an atomic war
wiping out the bulk of
mankind? It is true that I am
frightened, and deeply upset by
the thought—so deeply that I
have to ration myself how long
I think about it, no more than a
few seconds at a time. And I
guess most people are the same.

P.N. FURBANK

In other words, the fear of
death must be present behind
all our normal functioning in
order for the organism to be
armed toward self-preservation.
But the fear of death cannot be
present constantly in one's
mental faculties, else the
organism could not function.

ERNEST BECKER

It's impossible to experience one's own death objectively and still carry a tune.

WOODY ALLEN

I'm not afraid of death. It's the dying I'm afraid of, because we often lose dignity and control at the end of life. Our rights may be curtailed when we become someone's patient instead of a person. . . . Liberty, freedom, and privacy are cornerstones of our society and Constitution. Why should these be ignored at the end of life?

CAROL SCHRETER

If Jesus himself had told me that I wasn't going to die I wouldn't have believed Him. I was consumed by death. . . . I used to tell my parents, "if you care about me, pray that I won't wake up in the morning." I was afraid of dying but I wasn't afraid of being dead.

VIRGINIA ARTRU

You hit the mark, I said, the
fear of losing my life has stifled
all other pain.

JOHANN WOLFGANG VON GOETHE

To fear death because it is
unknown is hardly an
explanation. Fears are based on
an inner idea of helplessness. . . .
There is nothing intrinsically
frightening about the
"unknown." After all, we deal
with the unexpected and
unknown every day. We fear
the "unknown" only when we
have already invested it with
the mystery of death, not the
other way around.

AVERY WEISMAN

Usually, I would take to my heels and run until I was exhausted and panic stricken and would not grow calm again until I met another human being, the sight of whom would efface the agonizing sensation of the void that was gripping my heart.

NIKOLAI GOGOL

If after death we go on dreaming, if after death there is still something, then death (non-life) does not free us from the horror of being. Hamlet raises the question of being, not life. The horror of being.

MILAN KUNDERA

Men fear death as children fear to go in the dark; and as that natural fear in children is increased with tales, so is the other.

FRANCIS BACON

. . . I dreamed that Debbie and I were on a plane together that began to fall into the dingy evening light. I then dreamed that I awoke and grabbed Debbie, desperately hoping the crash was just a dream. But she wouldn't wake up, and, still dreaming, I began to race through the house only to find that both Jake and Casey were gone. I realized that Debbie and I were dead.

"We must be dead," I said aloud, "or the children would be here."

It was the first time that fear of death had ever penetrated that deeply into any dream I could remember.

ANDREW WARD

Since I was shot, everything is such a dream to me. I don't know what anything is about. Like I don't know whether I'm alive or whether I died. I wasn't afraid before and having been dead once, I shouldn't feel fear. But I'm afraid. I don't understand why.

ANDY WARHOL

They [truckers] were dangerous Speed Freaks driving twenty-ton trucks that might cut loose and jackknife at any moment, utterly out of control. There is nothing more terrifying than suddenly meeting a jackknifed Peterbilt with no brakes coming at you sideways at sixty or seventy miles per hour on a steep mountain road at three o'clock in the morning. There is a total understanding, all at once, of how the captain of the *Titanic* felt when he first saw the iceberg.

HUNTER S. THOMPSON

Bill had been shot at frequently. Once he had believed he was charmed too, but that feeling had ebbed from the moment he shot the policeman Mike Williams in Abilene. . . . Killing Mike Williams by accident told him he could be killed by accident too. And he was accordingly careful in places accidents happened. He never filled his right hand in a bar, he never sat with his back to the door.

PETE DEXTER

Since he had turned his back upon the fight, his fears had been wondrously magnified. Death about to thrust him between the shoulder-blades was far more dreadful than death about to smite him between the eyes. When he thought of it later, he conceived the impression that it is better to view the appalling than to be merely within hearing. The noises of the battle were like stones; he believed himself liable to be crushed.

STEPHEN CRANE

I used to drive to Edgemont Hospital in Hollywood for shock treatments in 1956. Every time I passed a funeral parlor I would be sure that there was no cigarette in my hand. I would also stop breathing until the traffic light changed and the car moved on. If anyone in the car spoke, I would become very disturbed physiologically. One of the funeral parlors has now been replaced, but I still observe my obeisance. I never look.

OSCAR LEVANT

I have a real terror of such things [funerals] and will not go.

SHIRLEY JACKSON

Neither for my sins of omission nor commission am I afraid of being punished. All that is past like a vision of Dante or Gustave Doré. My fear of God has settled down into a deep inward fear that my best offering may not prove acceptable in his sight. I'll tell you more about it in another world. . . .

ROBERT FROST

Coping

THE PHOBICS ANONYMOUS SYMBOL

THE EIGHT-SIDED OCTAGON is recognized as the universal stop sign. We in Phobics Anonymous chose this symbol to serve as a constant reminder that we must STOP catastrophic, negative, fearful thought processes and behaviors. We must STOP blaming people, places, and things for our problems and begin looking at our own reflection in the mirror.

THE BUTTERFLY at the top of the octagon symbolizes the freedom we experience upon working the 12 steps of Phobics Anonymous. It is the most human of all insects, for the pain of its metamorphosis most closely resembles the pain experienced in human growth, and the struggles which the Butterfly undergoes to emerge from its chrysalis is what gives the Butterfly the strength to live.

THE INITIALS "P.A." of Phobics Anonymous also serve as a devastating reminder of Panic Attacks which have given birth to the fellowship of Phobics Anonymous.

THE SOLID DOUBLE LINE around the octagon symbolizes the fact that we cannot do it alone. When we change the "me" to "we," we gain a sense of connection with the help of our Higher Power, to gain strength, become healthy, whole, and free.

For surely it is one thing quietly
to confess one's fear—and quite
another to give expression to it
unabashedly.

LUDWIG WITTGENSTEIN

. . . and so I have trained myself
to silence; induced to it also by
the terror I have of my own
unlimited capacity for feeling.

VIRGINIA WOOLF

For many men, fear is taboo,
something they keep secret
from girlfriends and wives. I am
not without friends, nor do I
think I am reluctant to admit a
fault, share a hope, or seek
advice on personal matters. But
I have always drawn the line at
sharing my fear.

THURSTON CLARKE

Once I realized that I'm phobic, that I don't have a brain tumor and I'm not going to die, I found I could manage.

ANONYMOUS PHOBIA PATIENT

Every man, of every age, entertains primal fears that must be faced or denied. We know the night monster must be wrestled to free us from those fears. Once grappled with, the monster flows through our fingers to vanish into the shadows. And we awake refreshed.

CLAIR REAS

Fear has to be acknowledged. We have to realize our fear and reconcile ourselves with fear. We should look at how we move, how we talk, how we conduct ourselves, how we chew our nails, how we sometimes put our hands in our pockets uselessly, then we will find something out about how fear is expressed in the form of restlessness. We must face the fact that fear is lurking in our lives, in everything we do.

CHOGYAM TRUNGPA

I am not afraid of anything. If you fear God you do not fear anything else.

MOAMMAR QADDAFI

They're [social phobics] afraid of dining in a restaurant or signing a check, because their hand might shake while holding a fork or pen and other people might notice and think badly of them.

Twenty percent of our patients with this disorder drank liquor before coming to see us for the first time. . . . They had to have a few drinks just to get here.

MICHAEL LIEBOWITZ
DIRECTOR OF THE ANXIETY CLINIC AT COLUMBIA PRESBYTERIAN MEDICAL CENTER

[Phobias] are not triggered by anything. One day—bang! —you wake up, and you're phobic. . . . Through repeated observations, I concluded that phobic reactions were usually connected to a problem in the stomach meridian. One of the treatment points for the stomach meridian is the second toe on both feet. Tapping both toes at the right spot balanced the flow of energy in the stomach meridian.

ROGER J. CALLAHAN

The pre-schizoid personality is generally called "schizoid effective," which means that as an adolescent he still hopes that he won't have to ask that cute chick (or boy) in the next row for a date. Speaking in terms of my own schizoid effective experience, one gazes at her for a year or so, mentally detailing all possible outcomes, the good ones go under the rubrick "daydreams" the bad ones under "phobia". . . . If the phobias win out (suppose I ask her and she says "with you?") the schizoid effective kid physically bolts from the classroom with agoraphobia that gradually widens into the schizophrenic avoidance of all human contact.

PHILIP K. DICK

Our tragedy today is a general and universal physical fear so long sustained by now that we can even bear it. There are no longer problems of the spirit. There is only the question: When will I be blown up? The basest of all things is to be afraid.

WILLIAM FAULKNER

He who is afraid of leaves must not come in the woods.

FRENCH PROVERB

We operate in this world as if we were protected by a glass bubble, and for some people panic is the first reaction to realizing there is no bubble; and that's when people buy guns.

CASANDRA THOMAS

I wear a piece of valuable jewelry that belongs to a friend. The totally irrational thinking behind this is that I can't crash— because I have to return my friend's ring, brooch, or whatever: it will save me. I consciously resist any attempt at relaxation: the totally irrational "magical thinking" that informs this behavior is that the moment I allow myself to relax the plane will crash! If I remain tense, I will be rewarded with a safe landing.

BARBARA GRIZZUTI HARRISON

I developed an unfortunate habit on airplanes, which always made me uneasy anyway. When I got on board, I'd swallow about six tranquilizers and sleeping pills and wash them down with booze provided so willingly by the stewardesses. My objective was to sleep through the trip and make it nonpainful.

The problem was that every once in a while the plane landed and the stewardesses couldn't wake me up.

SID CAESAR

If you don't worry about the guy you think might hurt you, you'll find that he *can't* hurt you. I was a little afraid at first, but I found there was nothing to be afraid of. As soon as I realized that those fears were all in my head, I knew they really didn't exist at all. Now I don't have them any more.

JIM PIERSALL

There are moments when a patient needs to be told that the breakdown, fear of which is wrecking his life, has already occurred. Similarly, it seems, for the lover's anxiety, it is the fear of a mourning that has already occurred, at the very origin of love, from the moment when I was first "ravished" someone would have to be able to tell me—"Don't be anxious anymore—you've already lost him/her."

ROLAND BARTHES

Look. We're just like everybody else, only quicker to pick up a danger. That's what makes an actor in the first place. That little rap of panic in the chest. We develop techniques to shield us from the facts. But they become the facts. The fear is so deep we find it waiting in the smallest role. We can't meet death on our own terms. We have no terms. Our speeches rattle in our throats. We're robbed of all consolations.

DON DE LILLO

The first duty of man is that of subduing fear.

THOMAS CARLYLE

To defend one's self against fear is simply to insure that one will, one day, be conquered by it; fears must be faced.

JAMES BALDWIN

So the biggest laughs are based on the biggest disappointments and the biggest fears.

KURT VONNEGUT

It's okay to feel it [fear], just don't show it.

ELVIS PRESLEY

Harnessing Fear

Fear is the beginning of wisdom.

WILLIAM TECUMSEH SHERMAN

Normal fear protects us; abnormal fear paralyzes us. Normal fear motivates us to improve our individual and collective welfare; abnormal fear constantly poisons and distorts our inner lives. Our problem is not to be rid of fear but, rather to harness and master it.

MARTIN LUTHER KING, JR.

What unites people very often is their fear.

BRUCE SPRINGSTEEN

It is not power that corrupts but fear. Fear of losing power corrupts those who wield it and fear of the scourge of power corrupts those who feel subject to it.

AUNG SAN SUU KYI

Our fears do make us traitors.

WILLIAM SHAKESPEARE

Neither a man, nor a crowd, nor a nation can be trusted to act humanely or to think sanely under the influence of a great fear.

BERTRAND RUSSELL

. . . and fear, by its nature is the enemy of thought.

HAROLD LASKI

Passion, prejudice, fears, neurosis spring from ignorance and take the form of myths and illusions.

ISAIAH BERLIN

Every person must live in fear and trembling, and therefore no established order may be free of fear and trembling. . . . Fear and trembling means there is a God, which no individual and no established order dare forget for an instant.

SØREN KIERKEGAARD

Among the earlier and simple phases of thought, two stand conspicuous—fear and greed. Fear, which by stimulating the imagination, creates a belief in an invisible world and develops a priesthood; and greed which dissipates energy in war and trade.

BROOKS ADAMS

Fear is an instructor of great sagacity and the herald of all revolution.

RALPH WALDO EMERSON

Where there is fear there is no religion.

MAHATMA GANDHI

Fear created Gods.

JOHN DEWEY

The thing we fear we bring to pass.

ELBERT HUBBARD

You know, you know, you
know, you know we can't
distinguish between *anxiety* and
fear. Do you know what I
mean? I don't mean fear.
I mean, I *do* mean "fear," I, I
don't mean *anxiety*. (Pause.)
        We . . . when we *fear*
things I think that we *wish* for
them. (Pause.) *Death*. Or
"burglars." (Pause.) Don't you
think? We mean we *wish* they
would come. Every fear hides a
wish. Don't you think?

DAVID MAMET

The thing most feared in secret
always happens; all it needs is a
little courage.

CESARE PAVESE

. . . if we must choose between them, it is far safer to be feared than to be loved.

NICCOLÒ MACHIAVELLI

Manson . . . preached that fear was beautiful, he often told the Family that they should live in a constant state of fear. . . . To Charlie fear was the same thing as awareness. . . . Manson would seek out each individual's greatest fear—not so the person could confront and eliminate it, but so he could re-emphasize it. It was like a magic button, which he could push at will to control that person.

VINCENT BUGLIOSI

My father was frightened of his mother, I was frightened by my father, and I'm damned well going to see to it that my children are frightened of me.

GEORGE V

Perhaps we have a deep need for these false fears, halfway between reality and playacting and games, the fear of mice, ranunculi, and spiders. They are our way of falling into line with tradition, providing ourselves to be the children of the culture in which we have grown up; or perhaps they help us relegate to the shadows other closer and vaster fears.

PRIMO LEVI

Generally, we associated "phobias" with isolated, irrational fears—a fear of a bridge, for example, or heights. But it's also a general style of being in the world: it's a need to make your world cozy and secure and utterly without risk.

JUDITH SILLS

I like to be frightened—I don't like to be revolted. . . . The imagination can create greater horror than we can ever show on the screen or in a book.

WILLIAM NOLAN

There is no delight the equal of dread.

CLIVE BARKER

Asked what scares her, one woman replied, "the shower scene in 'Psycho,' I've seen it twenty times."

KATHLEEN DOHENY

There is no hope without some fear, no fear without some hope.

BARUCH SPINOZA

Index of Names